My King James Bible Companion Series:

A Closer Look At

"SUPER CAPS"

In The King James Holy Bible

KEVIN MANN,
A Saved, King James Bible Believing Baptist

A closer look at

"SUPER CAPS"

IN THE KING JAMES HOLY BIBLE

Preface:

The King James AV 1611 Holy Bible (referred to from here on as "the bible") is God breathed, inerrant, (without proven error) supernatural, perfect, and superior to any other piece of literature ever written. There is not another book like it in the world! God has given us his word and words in the English which is the last universal world language just before the Second Coming of the great God and Saviour Jesus Christ. The Holy Spirit has reemphasized this truth in my heart and mind countless times since being born again in April 1972. It is "The Scripture" and all other "per-versions" are Satan's attempt to pull the wool over the eyes of lazy sheep who will not "Study to shew themselves approved unto God..." (2Tim 2:15) nor will they "Search the scripture..." (John 5:39) but they have willfully fallen victim to the little g "god" of this world, Satan, who blinds the eyes of anyone he can, always bringing doubt and questions in the mind of people concerning the truthfulness and integrity of the word and words of God. Gen. 3:1 "Yea, hath God said...?"

This paper is being written with the intent to highlight one of the marvelous "coincidences", as illiterate scoffers would say, found in the text of the bible than is often overlooked by the casual reader and most assuredly it is overlooked by Greek or Hebrew scholars who thinks that they are smart enough to correct God's word.

This phenomenon is the placement of words that appear in the bible that are written with all BLOCK CAPITAL letters or what I call "SUPER CAPS". There are twenty five of these occurrences found in the bible and they create their own message within the book of God. They appear "randomly" (Bible believers know that there is nothing random about the word of God, the Lord has it mapped out beautifully) throughout the Bible and number anywhere from one to thirteen words in the cluster.

My prayer for you is that this brief paper on the subject will be a benefit to you and will intensify your love for God's word, the King James Holy Bible.

Kevin Mann,
A Saved, King James Bible Believing Baptist,
@2013

KEVIN MANN

Books by this author:

FIRST MENTION-The first appearance of every word in the Bible laid out chronologically for easy bible marking.

FIRST MENTION NUGGETS

NEW TESTAMENT GIVING

JESUS IN GENESIS - JOESPH

ESTHER – A CLOSER LOOK

ISAIAH - MIRROR OF THE BIBLE

SUPER CAPS

TRIPLETS IN REVELATION

ONE TIME-words that only appear once in the scripture laid out in chronological order for easy bible marking.

NUMBER-WORD PLACEMENT-all numbers that appear in the verse at that exact number location, example: Seven is the seventh word in the verse.

NUMBER NUGGETS: NUMBERS ONE-FIVE
NUMBER NUGGETS: NUMBER SIX
NUMBER NUGGETS: NUMBER SEVEN
NUMBER NUGGETS: NUMBER EIGHT
NUMBER NUGGETS: NUMBER NINE
NUMBER NUGGETS: NUMBER TWELVE
NUMBER NUGGETS: NUMBER THIRTEEN

MY KING JAMES BIBLE COMPANION SERIES

A closer look at the

"SUPER CAPS"

In the King James Holy Bible

"Super Caps" are words or clusters of words that show up in the scripture in ALL BLOCK CAPITAL LETTERS, every reference to the word "scripture" or "the bible" is referring to the only true perfect word of God, the King James AV 1611 Holy Bible, (I know that the Laodicean "Christians" don't believe that statement but that's because they don't spend any time in the book and they are lazy, stupid, self willed, carnal and wish to be their own "final authority" instead of allowing God and his word to be their final authority, you're welcome.)

The Bible displays twenty five occurrences of **"Super Caps"** throughout the scriptures; some contain only one word while others contain several words.

Eleven of the occurrences are references to God the Father,

Eleven of the occurrences are references to God the Son,

And three of them, when read in their immediate context where they appear, refer to Satan's five thousand year old false religious whore bride who is still masquerading around as a "church" (Catholic, just so you know) and claiming to be "The

True Church" (Catholic, just so there is no chance of you mistaking or misunderstanding to who I am referring) she is the whore of Babylon and she is even to this day carrying on the practices, rites, and traditions of the religious system from which it was birthed back in Gen. 10:10 under Nimrod in the first kingdom mentioned in the Bible, **Babel**, (Babylon in the plains of Shinar as we know it in scripture). The Babylonian whore religion comes complete with vestal virgins (nuns), black robed priests who are called "Father", the worship of the "Queen of Heaven, (Jer. 44:17-25 called "Mary" by the modern day worshippers of "Baal-Ashtoreth" (13 letters, Jud. 2:13, 10:6) incense, idols, "saints", a "holy papa" and a false "bible" which is Satan's counterfeit manuscripts from a Catholic monastery in Alexandria Egypt (type of the world), from where we got the RSV and all of the perversions that come from it such as the ASV, the NASV, the NIV and the New King "Jimmie".

When these twenty five supper caps are read as they appear in the Bible they take on their own true significance. A tremendous message buried within the text of the Holy Scriptures. Read the list over a few times before proceeding to get the full impact of what God is saying to us using just the "super caps" embedded in the Bible.

First is the chronological appearance of the "Super Caps" as they are in the Holy Bible. This list appears again later with the reference addresses:

I AM THAT I AM, I AM

JEHOVAH

HOLINESS TO THE LORD

HOLINESS TO THE LORD

THE LORD THY GOD

JAH

JEHOVAH

JEHOVAH

JEHOVAH

THE LORD OUR RIGHTEOUSNESS

MENE, MENE, TEKEL, UPHARSIN, MENE; TEKEL; PERES:

the **BRANCH**

the **BRANCH**

HOLINESS UNTO THE LORD

JESUS

JESUS

THIS IS THE KING OF THE JEWS

THE KING OF THE JEWS

JESUS

JESUS

THIS IS THE KING OF THE JEWS

JESUS OF NAZARETH THE KING OF THE JEWS

TO THE UNKNOWN GOD

MYSTERY, BABYLON THE GREAT, THE MOTHER OF HARLOTS AND ABOMINATIONS OF THE EARTH

KING OF KINGS AND LORD OF LORDS

What a message within the Bible just reading the super caps

as they appear in the blessed word and words of God.

THE THREE GROUPS OF NEGATIVE CAPS

First I want to wade into the cesspool, muck, and mire of the three NEGATIVE references in the list, these are connected to Satan's false religious system, both the spiritual [Whore Church in Rev.] and physical [the pagan Babylonians in Dan. 5] these two kingdoms are a counterfeit of God's two kingdoms [spiritual, the kingdom of God and physical, the kingdom of heaven] then we will come back up to the surface for a breath of fresh air. The three groups of the negative "super caps" that we will discuss are found in Daniel 5, Acts 17, and Rev. 17 they are unmistakably "connected at the hip".

I would like to begin with the super caps found in Rev. 17 because they represent the culmination of the religion of Satan, the whore of Babylon, then we will connect Daniel and Acts to her looking backward into the Bible.

Turn to Rev. 17:5, **MYSTERY, BABYLON THE GREAT, THE MOTHER OF HARLOTS AND ABOMINATIONS OF THE EARTH**

Here we have a set of super caps which are the unmistaken description of the **church**, the **bride**, and the **city** of Satan who is called in the scripture Mystery Babylon, the Great Whore. She is given the name of "The Whore" and her "name" is written on her forehead, just as the Antichrist will place his mark in the foreheads of all of the people in the tribulation period who worship the beast.

Her name consists of **13** words (count them) containing a

total of **65** (5x13) letters. It is no accident that the name of the church of Satan contains the multiples of the number **thirteen** for the number thirteen in scripture has a negative connotation 85% of the time and you can't get more negative than the prince of darkness. For an example of thirteen as a negative number we need to look at the **first place** in scripture where two thirteen's collide that is Gen. "**13:13**", the verse has **13** words and it is forever connected with "Sodom-Gomorrah" (**13** letters), "homosexuality" (**13** letters). There are 2 words that appear for the very first time in scripture they are "wicked-sinners" (**13** letters), and just by sheer coincidence (yeah, right) the sodomites were destroyed by "fire-brimstone" **13** letters in Gen. 19:24. Therefore the number 13 is forever connected in scripture with the sin of homosexuality, evil, rebellion, sin, rebellion, perversion, destruction, and wickedness this observation holds up consistently negative 85% of the time throughout the scripture.

In Rev.17 we have the face of Satan's five thousand year old false religion represented by a female who is said to be a whore and the mother of all whores who is still to this day masquerading around as a universal "church" (today it is called "Catholic", same whore, just a new name so you know of whom I speak) and claiming to be "the true Church" (Catholic, just so there is no chance of you mistaking or misunderstanding to who I am referring) she is the whore of Babylon and she is carrying on all of the practices, rites, rituals and traditions and perversions of the pagan religious system reaching all the way back to Gen. 10:10 under Nimrod in the first kingdom mentioned in the Bible, **Babel**, (Babylon in the plains of Shinar as we know it in scripture and as it exists today, read "Babylon, Mystery Religion", Woodrow 1966 and The Two Babylons by Hislop). The Babylonian whore religion parades around today just as it did under Nimrod five thousand years ago complete with a harem of temple prostitutes, "perpetual virgins" (nuns), black robed priests who dress like "mommas" and are called "papas", who worship the "Queen of Heaven, (Jer. 44:17-25 called "Mary" by the modern day worshippers of "Baal-

Ashtoreth" (13 letters, Jud. 2:13, 10:6 male and female deities propagating sexual perversion) with their incense, idols, a "holy papa", sexual perversions (predominantly pedophilia and sodomy) based on a set of false "manuscripts" which were used to produced Satan's counterfeit bible beginning with the corrupt manuscripts found in Alexandria Egypt (type of the world) and continuing on to 1895, the RSV, and all of the perversions that came from it such as the ASV, the NASV, NEB, NJB, NWT, the NIV and the New King "Jimmie" per-Version.

The Mystery Whore in Rev. 17 is Satan's "bride" which is a counterfeit of the Lord Jesus Christ's pure chaste virgin bride (2Cor.11:2), a counterfeit of Christ's city, New Jerusalem (Rev.21), and a counterfeit of the real Church, the body of Christ (Eph.4:4). She commits fornication with any and every false religion, king (vs.2) and inhabitant of the earth and she makes them drunk with the wine of her fornication, she is a whore and that's what whores do. The power she has over the masses of ignorant religionists is staggering. Her colors are "scarlet-purple" (**13** letters), she is decked with silver, gold, precious stones and pearls" (vs.4 she loves her opulence) she drinks the blood of the saints and the martyrs of Jesus (vs.6) out of her symbol which is a golden cup, along with her filthiness and fornication and she sits on seven mountains (Rome, religious Babylon vs. 9).

What a great wife you have there Saint Satan, she is very becoming of you, a great compliment to your existence. Rev. 17:18 (3x6) "**And the woman which thou sawest IS that great city, which reigneth over the kings of the earth**", she is a religious and political system under the control of her husband Satan, the king of terrors. (Job 18:14)

Just for fun I am including a list of a few phrases that are connected closely with the pagan practices of Mystery Babylon. All of them have something in common; see if you can figure out the connection. Read them carefully.

*Roman Catholic, *purple-scarlet, *Queen of Heaven (Jer.44:17), *Christmas Tree (Jer. 10), *Easter Egg Hunt, *Saint Nicholas, *Roman Soldiers, *King of Babylon, *The Golden City, *The Antichrist, *false brethren, *false teachers, *false prophets, *false apostles, *Baal-Ashtoreth, *false doctrine, *false religion, *Judas Iscariot, *Prince of Tyrus, *unclean spirit, *bottomless pit, *Jacob's Trouble, and *blood of saints.

Do you see what they have in common? They all contain **13 letters**. And you think this is a coincidence do you? Yeah Right!

THE SECOND GROUP OF NEGATIVE CAPS IS FOUND IN ACTS 17:23

TO THE UNKNOWN GOD

Now let's turn to the second group of negative "Super Caps" that are found in the Book of Acts 17:23 (just as the passage in Revelation 17) here Paul is speaking to the **"idolatrous city"** (in other words a "religious" city just like the city of the great whore Babylon.) of Athens, Greece. Paul addresses the religious, superstitious philosophers known as the Epicureans and the Stoics on Mars' hill and he says in verse 23, "For as I passed by, and behold your **"devotions"** (a religious activity) I found an **altar** (a religious item) with this inscription, **TO THE UNKNOWN GOD**. (a religious deity) Whom therefore ye ignorantly **worship**, (a religious activity) him declare I unto you" so you can see that these words were spoken by the Apostle Paul to a city full of lost, idol worshipping, religious pagans (straight out of Rome, the connection is undeniable) and he uses this inscription to declare to them the one true God, the Lord Jesus Christ, who was "unknown" to the sinners in Athens. The one whom these religious people ignorantly worshipped, just to cover their "spiritual" bases, Paul declared as the true living God. Even though this inscription was not intended by the Athenians as a reference to the true God (as I numbered them in the preface) Paul made the brilliant application to the God of heaven and earth in his delivery to them. Here again, just as the super caps in Rev.17 we have the same crowd of religious pagans that are connected to Satan's false religious system dating back five thousand years to Nimrod. The entire Roman Empire was influenced by the religions and customs of the peoples that they conquered. The Romans were multi-god worshipping pagans whose religion included all sorts of sexual immorality and perversion in their "worship" services, feasts and daily activities and the city of Athens was no exception as we see Paul dealing with the community leaders. Only the Lord Jesus Christ can deliver a soul from the "religion" of Rome as the men of Athens are soon to learn.

THE THIRD GROUP OF NEGATIVE CAPS ARE FOUND IN DAN 5:25-27.

MENE, MENE, TEKEL, UPHARSIN, MENE; TEKEL; PERES:

Our third group of negative "super caps" shows up in the list thirteen places before the Whore of Babylon of Rev. 17, these words were a supernatural message given to, who else? the king of Babylon who is a type of Satan and he is warned of his impending overthrow and doom. This warning is also applicable to all of lost mankind!

Dan. 5:25-27, **MENE, MENE, TEKEL, UPHARSIN, MENE; TEKEL; PERES:** 7 words

"God hath numbered thy kingdom, and finished it… Thou art weighed in the balances, and art found wanting." (A loose New Testament application of the handwriting on the wall could be: "For all have sinned and come short of the glory of God; Rom. 3:23, which is applicable to every man, woman, boy and girl alive today.)

Read the entire chapter and notice the context, Belshazzar the king of Babylon, the grandson of Nebuchadnezzar (a type of Satan) who captured the Jews and destroyed Jerusalem in 606 B.C., (as the Antichrist will do in the Great Tribulation period in 20??) is conducting a drunken "religious" orgy (FYI nakedness, sex and booze always go hand in hand and are two sides of the same ungodly coin just as the modern day Baal worshippers can testify) in the Palace at Babylon which is the seat of the false religious idolatrous worship of Baal. He is entertaining a thousand of his lords, his wives, and his concubines (mistresses) and right in the middle of a great "religious worship service" (the scripture says that they were "praising the gods of silver", while "defiling the gold vessels" taken from the Jewish Temple in Jerusalem by Nebuchadnezzar, that's Satan's idea of a great worship service, debauchery and blasphemy) everything changes as the fingers of a man's hand (the man Christ Jesus) appears over against the wall and writes a message in the sight of the drunken fornicators while (in the middle of the festivities) they indulge in their idolatrous orgy (that's the same way that God is going to appear to the lost man, when he does it will be sudden and unexpected, right in the middle of their "living it up" and while holding to their weak, powerless religion).

In Dan. 5:6 is the picture of what every lost, hell bound sinner will experience when they are confronted with God's words at the Great White Throne Judgment (Rev. 20:11). Their countenance will change (from drunken, sensual pleasure to pure horror), his thoughts will trouble him, (Oh my God, that loud mouth preacher was right, what am I going to do now?) and his knees smote (knocked) one against the other, and then they will cry aloud...OH MY GOD!! Bring me my horoscope, where are my scientists, my philosophers, my preacher, my priest and my holy papa! This is the horror that every hell bound sinner will face when his time comes unexpectedly to meet God. They will be "greatly troubled" vs. 9 their countenance will change and they will be astonied (old English, as a stone, speechless, astonished).

Here in Dan. 5:25-27 we see the seven "words" that God wrote on the wall with the fingers of a man's hand, it truly is a warning to all sinners but specifically in the context it is the demise of Satan's whore bride the false religion of Babylon.

MENE, MENE, TEKEL, UPHARSIN, MENE; TEKEL; PERES:

Thou art weighed in the balances and art found <u>wanting</u> (old English, lacking).

Thy kingdom is divided...

This can be applied to every lost man and woman as: "For all have sinned and come short of the glory of God; Rom. 3:23) This is every sinner's problem they are found wanting when weighed in the balances of God's righteousness, for our "goodness" will not to be compared to the goodness of "other sinners" if that were the case we would all make it to heaven but we will be weighed in the balances of God's righteousness against the Lord Jesus Christ who is God in the flesh and who is perfect and sinless. When God gets through weighing you there will be no doubt in your mind or the mind of every sinner there that his judgment and their condemnation is just. (Rom. 3:26)

This message doctrinally is addressed to Satan the husband of the great religious and pagan whore system of Babylon through Belshazzar, the king of Babylon, (see context of Dan. 5) because it is Satan's "religious kingdom" that will ultimately be divided and fall at the Second Coming of the Lord Jesus Christ (Rev. 14:8, Babylon the great is fallen, is fallen, that great city.) just a coincidence? Bible believers know that there is no such thing as a coincidence in the King James Holy Bible. That book is supernatural and it is fearfully and wonderfully made.

NOW FOR SOME FRESH AIR!

I Am Alpha and Omega the "Bookends" of the Bible Super Caps.

The most remarkable "super caps" in the Bible to me is the "Alpha and Omega" the "first and last", the "beginning and the end" of the list of words. The **first** group of "super caps" in the scripture just happens to be God's name, and contains 7 (perfection or complete) words and is found in Ex.3:14, the last group of "super caps" in the scripture is also God's name containing 7 words found and they are found in Rev.19:16. Reading the two names of God together you read God declaring:

I AM THAT I AM, I AM – KING OF KINGS AND LORD OF LORDS

Amen! Holy "bookends", God the Father and God the Son forever connected across 6000 years of human history in the first 7-word super caps, and the last 7-word super caps in the King James Holy Bible. They not only forever connect the Godhead (the Father and the Son as one in the same) but they also connect both the Old and the New Testaments together as one book. They also connect both kingdoms, the kingdom of God, (spiritual), and the kingdom of Heaven, (physical). The Lord Jesus Christ and the God of Heaven and Earth are **one in the same** and the Bible, made up of sixty-six separate books, is in truth just **one book** and it is as seamless and as easily read as the fourteen word statement above,

I AM THAT I AM, I AM - KING OF KINGS AND LORD OF LORDS.

That book you've got a hold of there is some hot ticket bud! There is not another one like it on the face of the Earth! ANYWHERE! Most lazy, carnal, English speaking "Christians" (and I use that term loosely) don't even have a clue as to the significance of what they just read, nor do they appreciate what God has given them in the reformation Bible that I hold in my hands the King James AV 1611 Holy Bible. My God, if that bible were any more perfect it would get up and walk around!!!!

More on the - "I AM" connection!

The Lord Jesus Christ, in the Gospel of John, made **eight** (number for new beginnings) definitive statements beginning with "I AM" thus connecting himself to and declaring himself to be equal with 'Jehovah' (7 letters), 'The LORD' (7 letters), 'the LORD' (7 letters).

In John 6:35, he said "I am the bread of life", in 8:12, "I am the light of the world", in 10:7, "I am the door", in 10:11, "I am the good shepherd", in 10:36 "I am the Son of God" in 11:25, "I am the resurrection", in 14:6, "I am the way, the truth, and the life", and in 15:1, He said "I am the true vine".

The Lord also stated in Rev. 1:8 (also penned by the Apostle John) "I am the Alpha and Omega, the beginning and the end, which is and which was, and which is to come, the Almighty." in Rev. 1:17-18, he said "I am the first and the last: I am he that liveth and was dead and behold I am alive for evermore". In the Garden of Gethsemane when Judas betrayed the Lord and brought the soldiers to take him and in John 18:4-6 "he said unto them, Whom seek ye? ... I am he... As soon as he had said unto them, I am he, they went backward, and fell to the ground." Just the words "I AM" spoken by the Lord Jesus Christ knocked his enemies to the ground in the garden prior to his arrest, and mock kangeroo trial.

In John 8:58 the Lord Jesus told the Jews ..."Before Abraham was I AM", he claimed himself to be the Great I Am, the God of Heaven and Earth, the LORD God Jehovah, so they proceeded to stone him, there is no question as to who the Lord Jesus claimed to be so much as the Jews plotted his destruction and death.

In John 4, the Lord told the woman at the well, "I that speak to thee am he (the Messiah). Without question Jesus declared himself as God in the flesh, the great I AM.

All of the "super caps", their number in the line-up as they appear (1 to 25), and the place (context) in the scripture where they appear is no accident, there are no accidents or coincidences in the word of God. Take a look at the words in Ex.3, "I AM THAT I AM, I AM". Here in chapter **three** we have a total of **seven** words that are made up of only **three** separate words, I and AM and THAT, (3 words) the other words I and AM are a repeat of the first two words for a total of **three** times. The words I and AM are made up of **three** different letters, and those three letters are repeated **three** times total so you have the **Trinity** represented. Three separate words repeated three times consisting of three I's, three A's and three M's, even a fourth grade boys Sunday School class in a Bible believing youth department could see the significance of all of these three's, **IT IS THE TRINITY!**

I AM THAT I AM, I AM, (He is the Alpha, the First, the Beginning, the starting in Exodus)

KING OF KINGS AND LORD OF LORDS, (He is the Omega, the Last, the Ending, the finishing up in Revelation) God's blessed holy name, the bookends of Super Caps if you please.

Now we will list the Super Caps as they appear chronologically in the Bible with their addresses along with some other particular observations of the groups themselves.

Ex. 3:14, **I AM THAT I AM, I AM;**
Here, the first appearance of super caps in the Bible is fittingly God's name. The first super cap phrase contains a total of 7 words. 7 is the number for completion or perfection.
Two of the words contain a total of only 3 letters, and those 3 letters are repeated 3 times. 'I AM, I AM, I AM'.

There is a total of 3 different words in the phrase – 'I AM THAT'- these "three threes" denote the Trinity itself in the name because God is a trinity, the Godhead includes; God the Father, God the Son, and God the Holy Ghost.

Three in ONE and ONE in Three, and the ONE in the middle died for me. The trinity is not $1+1+1=3$, but $1 \times 1 \times 1 = 1$

The second occurrence is:
Ex. 6:3, **JEHOVAH;** God's name containing 7 letters.

The third is;
Ex. 28:36, **HOLINESS TO THE LORD.** Inscription on the crown of the High Priest

The fourth is;
Ex. 39:30, **HOLINESS TO THE LORD;** The inscription that is found on the crown of the High Priest.

The fifth is;
Dt. 28:58, **THE LORD THY GOD;** God's name

The sixth is;
Ps. 68:4, **JAH;** God's name containing 3 letters (the number of the Trinity)

The seventh is;
Ps. 83:18, **JEHOVAH;** God's name, 7 letters.

The eighth is;
Isa. 12:2, **JEHOVAH;** God's name, 7 letters

The ninth is;
Isa. 26:4, **JEHOVAH;** God's name, 7 letters

The tenth;
Jer. 23:6, **THE LORD OUR RIGHTEOUSNESS;** God's name

The eleventh is;
Dan. 5:25-27 **MENE, MENE, TEKEL, UPHARSIN, MENE; TEKEL; PERES:** 7 words (A loose interpretation could be: "For all have sinned and come short of the glory of God; Rom. 3:23)

The twelfth;
Zech. 3:8, the **BRANCH;** referring to the Lord Jesus Christ

The thirteenth;
Zech. 6:12, the **BRANCH**, the Lord Jesus Christ

The fourteenth;
Zech. 14:20, **HOLINESS UNTO THE LORD;** Inscription on the bells on the horses' bridles in the Millennium.

The fifteenth;
Mat. 1:21, **JESUS;** God's name in the flesh

The sixteenth;
Mat. 1:25, **JESUS;** God's name in the flesh

The seventeenth;
Mat. 27:37, **THIS IS THE KING OF THE JEWS;** 7 words

The eighteenth;
Mk. 15:26, **THE KING OF THE JEWS;**

The nineteenth;
Luke 1:31, **JESUS;** God's name in the flesh

The twentieth;

Luke 2:21, **JESUS;** God's name in the flesh

The twenty-first;
Luke 23:38, **THIS IS THE KING OF THE JEWS;** 7 words

The twenty-second;
Jn. 19:19, **JESUS OF NAZARETH THE KING OF THE JEWS;**

The twenty-third;
Acts 17:23, **TO THE UNKNOWN GOD;**

The twenty-fourth;
Rev.17:5, **MYSTERY, BABYLON THE GREAT, THE MOTHER OF HARLOTS AND ABOMINATIONS OF THE EARTH;** 13 words with 65 (5x13) letters, the name of Satan's bride and his city.

The twenty-fifth, and last occurrence;
Rev. 19:16, **KING OF KINGS AND LORD OF LORDS** Jesus' name at his Second coming containing 7 words.

A breakdown of the occurrences:
There are eight (8 new beginning) specific names of **God the Father** in the list:
Ex. 3:14, **I AM THAT I AM, I AM**, 7 (perfect, complete) words.
Ex. 6:3, **JEHOVAH**, 7 letters
Dt. 28:58, **THE LORD THY GOD**, 13 letters
Ps. 68:4, **JAH**, 3 letters
Ps. 83:18, **JEHOVAH**, 7 letters
Isa. 12:2, **JEHOVAH**, 7 letters
Isa. 26:4, **JEHOVAH**, 7 letters
Jer. 23:6, **THE LORD OUR RIGHTEOUSNESS**

There are seven (perfect, complete) specific names of **God the Son**

in the list:
Zech. 3:8, the **BRANCH**
Zech. 6:12, the **BRANCH**
Mat. 1:21, **JESUS**
Mat. 1:25, **JESUS**
Luke 1:31, **JESUS**
Luke 2:21, **JESUS**
Rev. 19:16, **KING OF KINGS AND LORD OF LORDS;** 7 words

There was one (1) specific name on the forehead of the whore of Babylon in the list:
Rev.17:5; "**MYSTERY, BABYLON THE GREAT, THE MOTHER OF HARLOTS AND ABOMINATIONS OF THE EARTH**" 13 words containing 65 (5x13) letters describing Satan's bride; the whore of Babylon.

There are eight (8) inscriptions written on inanimate objects:

There are four (4) on the cross of Jesus in the gospels:
Mat. 27:37, **THIS IS THE KING OF THE JEWS** 7 words
Mk. 15:26, **THE KING OF THE JEWS**
Luke 23:38, **THIS IS THE KING OF THE JEWS** 7 words
Jn. 19:19, **JESUS OF NAZARETH THE KING OF THE JEWS**

Twice (2) referring to the plate of gold on the head of the High Priest in the Tabernacle:
Ex. 28:36, **HOLINESS TO THE LORD**
Ex. 39:30, **HOLINESS TO THE LORD**

One (1) written on the wall:
Dan. 25-27 **MENE, MENE, TEKEL, UPHARSIN, MENE; TEKEL; PERES:** 7 words

One (1) on the altar in Athens:
Acts 17:23, **TO THE UNKNOWN GOD**.

The dispensational placement according to the context in which they are found:

The Tribulation:
Dt. 28:58, **THE LORD THY GOD**
Ps. 83:18, **JEHOVAH**
Dan. 5:25-27, **MENE, MENE, TEKEL, UPHARSIN, MENE; TEKEL; PERES:**
Rev.17:5, **MYSTERY, BABYLON THE GREAT, THE MOTHER OF HARLOTS AND ABOMINATIONS OF THE EARTH**

The Second Advent:
Ps. 68:4, **JAH**
Rev. 19:16, **KING OF KINGS AND LORD OF LORDS**

The Millennium:
Ex. 6:3, **JEHOVAH**
Isa. 12:2, **JEHOVAH**
Isa. 26:4, **JEHOVAH**
Jer. 23:6, **THE LORD OUR RIGHTEOUSNESS**
Zech. 3:8, the **BRANCH**
Zech. 6:12, the **BRANCH**
Zech. 14:20, **HOLINESS UNTO THE LORD**

Under the Law, before Jesus died on the cross
Mat. 1:21, **JESUS**
Mat. 1:25, **JESUS**
Mat. 27:37, **THIS IS THE KING OF THE JEWS**
Mk. 15:26, **THE KING OF THE JEWS**
Luke 1:31, **JESUS**
Luke 2:21, **JESUS**
Luke 23:38, **THIS IS THE KING OF THE JEWS**
Jn. 19:19, **JESUS OF NAZARETH THE KING OF THE JEWS**

The King James AV 1611 Holy Bible is God breathed, inerrant, supernatural, perfect, and superior to any other piece of literature ever written. There is not another book like it in the world! God has given us his word and words in the English which is the last universal world language just before the Second Coming of the great God and Savior Jesus Christ. The Holy Spirit has reemphasized this truth in my heart and mind countless times since being born again in April 1972. It is "The Scripture" and all other "per-versions" are Satan's attempt to pull the wool over the eyes of lazy sheep who will not "Study to shew themselves approved unto God..." (2Tim 2:15) nor will they "Search the scripture..." (John 5:39) but they have willfully fallen victim to the little g "god" of this world, Satan, who blinds the eyes of anyone he can, always bringing doubt and questions in the mind of people concerning the truthfulness and integrity of the word and words of God. Gen. 3:1 "Yea, hath God said...?"

Super Caps in the King James Holy Bible. What a book!

KEVIN MANN
A Saved, King James Bible Believing Baptist.

Made in the USA
Columbia, SC
04 July 2025